Great Works

Instructional Guides for Literature

THE CROSSOVER

A guide for the novel by Kwame Alexander
Great Works Author: Angela Johnson, M.A.Ed., M.F.A.

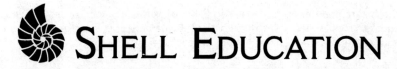

SHELL EDUCATION

Contributing Authors

Emily R. Smith, M.A.Ed.; Brian McGrath (page 12), and Kiley Smith (poem on page 66)

Publishing Credits

Corinne Burton, M.A.Ed., *President*; Emily R. Smith, M.A.Ed., *Content Director*; Lee Aucoin, *Multimedia Designer*; Stephanie Bernard, *Assistant Editor*; Don Tran, *Graphic Designer*

Image Credits

iStock (cover)

Standards

© 2007 Teachers of English to Speakers of Other Languages, Inc. (TESOL)
© 2007 Board of Regents of the University of Wisconsin System. World-Class Instructional Design and Assessment (WIDA)
© Copyright 2010. National Governors Association Center for Best Practices and Council of Chief State School Officers. All rights reserved.

Shell Education

a division of Teacher Created Materials
5301 Oceanus Drive
Huntington Beach, CA 92649-1030
ISBN 978-1-4258-1648-3
https://www.tcmpub.com/shell-education
© 2017 Shell Educational Publishing, Inc.

Table of Contents

How to Use This Literature Guide 4
  Theme Thoughts 4
  Vocabulary 5
  Analyzing the Literature 6
  Reader Response 6
  Close Reading the Literature 6
  Making Connections 7
  Creating with the Story Elements 7
  Culminating Activity 8
  Comprehension Assessment 8
  Response to Literature 8

Correlation to the Standards 8
  Purpose and Intent of Standards 8
  How to Find Standards Correlations 8
  Standards Correlation Chart 9
  TESOL and WIDA Standards 10

About the Author—Kwame Alexander 11
  Possible Texts for Text Comparisons 11

Book Summary of *The Crossover* 12
  Cross-Curricular Connection 12
  Possible Texts for Text Sets 12

Teacher Plans and Student Pages 13
  Pre-Reading Theme Thoughts 13
  Section 1: Warm-Up 14
  Section 2: First Quarter 24
  Section 3: Second Quarter 34
  Section 4: Third Quarter 44
  Section 5: Fourth Quarter and Overtime 54

Post-Reading Activities 64
  Post-Reading Theme Thoughts .64
  Culminating Activity: Summary and Verse Book Review 65
  Comprehension Assessment 67
  Response to Literature: *The Crossover* 69

Answer Key 71

How to Use This Literature Guide

Today's standards demand rigor and relevance in the reading of complex texts. The units in this series guide teachers in a rich and deep exploration of worthwhile works of literature for classroom study. The most rigorous instruction can also be interesting and engaging!

Many current strategies for effective literacy instruction have been incorporated into these instructional guides for literature. Throughout the units, text-dependent questions are used to determine comprehension of the book as well as student interpretation of the vocabulary words. The books chosen for the series are complex exemplars of carefully crafted works of literature. Close reading is used throughout the units to guide students toward revisiting the text and using textual evidence to respond to prompts orally and in writing. Students must analyze the story elements in multiple assignments for each section of the book. All of these strategies work together to rigorously guide students through their study of literature.

The next few pages will make clear how to use this guide for a purposeful and meaningful literature study. Each section of this guide is set up in the same way to make it easier for you to implement the instruction in your classroom.

Theme Thoughts

The great works of literature used throughout this series have important themes that have been relevant to people for many years. Many of the themes will be discussed during the various sections of this instructional guide. However, it would also benefit students to have independent time to think about the key themes of the novel.

Before students begin reading, have them complete *Pre-Reading Theme Thoughts* (page 13). This graphic organizer will allow students to think about the themes outside the context of the story. They'll have the opportunity to evaluate statements based on important themes and defend their opinions. Be sure to have students keep their papers for comparison to the *Post-Reading Theme Thoughts* (page 64). This graphic organizer is similar to the pre-reading activity. However, this time, students will be answering the questions from the point of view of one of the characters in the novel. They have to think about how the character would feel about each statement and defend their thoughts. To conclude the activity, have students compare what they thought about the themes before they read the novel to what the characters discovered during the story.

How to Use This Literature Guide (cont.)

Vocabulary

Each teacher overview page has definitions and sentences about how key vocabulary words are used in the section. These words should be introduced and discussed with students. There are two student vocabulary activity pages in each section. On the first page, students are asked to define the ten words chosen by the author of this unit. On the second page in most sections, each student will select at least eight words that he or she finds interesting or difficult. For each section, choose one of these pages for your students to complete. With either assignment, you may want to have students get into pairs to discuss the meanings of the words. Allow students to use reference guides to define the words. Monitor students to make sure the definitions they have found are accurate and relate to how the words are used in the text.

On some of the vocabulary student pages, students are asked to answer text-related questions about the vocabulary words. The following question stems will help you create your own vocabulary questions if you'd like to extend the discussion.

- How does this word describe _____'s character?
- In what ways does this word relate to the problem in this story?
- How does this word help you understand the setting?
- In what ways is this word related to the story's solution?
- Describe how this word supports the novel's theme of . . . .
- What visual images does this word bring to your mind?
- For what reasons might the author have chosen to use this particular word?

At times, more work with the words will help students understand their meanings. The following quick vocabulary activities are a good way to further study the words.

- Have students practice their vocabulary and writing skills by creating sentences and/or paragraphs in which multiple vocabulary words are used correctly and with evidence of understanding.
- Students can play vocabulary concentration. Students make a set of cards with the words and a separate set of cards with the definitions. Then, students lay the cards out on the table and play concentration. The goal of the game is to match vocabulary words with their definitions.
- Students can create word journal entries about the words. Students choose words they think are important and then describe why they think each word is important within the novel.

How to Use This Literature Guide *(cont.)*

Analyzing the Literature

After students have read each section, hold small-group or whole-class discussions. Questions are written at two levels of complexity to allow you to decide which questions best meet the needs of your students. The Level 1 questions are typically less abstract than the Level 2 questions. Level 1 is indicated by a square, while Level 2 is indicated by a triangle. These questions focus on the various story elements, such as character, setting, and plot. Student pages are provided if you want to assign these questions for individual student work before your group discussion. Be sure to add further questions as your students discuss what they've read. For each question, a few key points are provided for your reference as you discuss the novel with students.

Reader Response

In today's classrooms, there are often great readers who are below-average writers. So much time and energy is spent in classrooms getting students to read on grade level that little time is left to focus on writing skills. To help teachers include more writing in their daily literacy instruction, each section of this guide has a literature-based reader response prompt. Each of the three genres of writing is used in the reader responses within this guide: narrative, informative/explanatory, and opinion/argument. Students have a choice between two prompts for each reader response. One response requires students to make connections between the reading and their own lives. The other prompt requires students to determine text-to-text connections or connections within the text.

Close Reading the Literature

Within each section, students are asked to closely reread a short section of text. Since some versions of the novels have different page numbers, the selections are described by chapter and location, along with quotations to guide the readers. After each close reading, there are text-dependent questions to be answered by students.

Encourage students to read each question one at a time and then go back to the text and discover the answer. Work with students to ensure that they use the text to determine their answers rather than making unsupported inferences. Once students have answered the questions, discuss what they discovered. Suggested answers are provided in the answer key.

How to Use This Literature Guide (cont.)

Close Reading the Literature (cont.)

The generic, open-ended stems below can be used to write your own text-dependent questions if you would like to give students more practice.

- Give evidence from the text to support . . . .
- Justify your thinking using text evidence about . . . .
- Find evidence to support your conclusions about . . . .
- What text evidence helps the reader understand . . . ?
- Use the book to tell why _____ happens.
- Based on events in the story, ...
- Use text evidence to describe why . . . .

Making Connections

The activities in this section help students make cross-curricular connections to writing, mathematics, science, social studies, or the fine arts. Each of these types of activities requires higher-order thinking skills from students.

Creating with the Story Elements

It is important to spend time discussing the common story elements in literature. Understanding the characters, setting, and plot can increase students' comprehension and appreciation of the story. If teachers discuss these elements daily, students will more likely internalize the concepts and look for the elements in their independent reading. Another important reason for focusing on the story elements is that students will be better writers if they think about how the stories they read are constructed.

Students are given three options for working with the story elements. They are asked to create something related to the characters, setting, or plot of the novel. Students are given a choice in this activity so that they can decide to complete the activity that most appeals to them. Different multiple intelligences are used so that the activities are diverse and interesting to all students.

How to Use This Literature Guide (cont.)

Culminating Activity

This open-ended, cross-curricular activity requires higher-order thinking and allows for a creative product. Students will enjoy getting the chance to share what they have discovered through reading the novel. Be sure to allow them enough time to complete the activity at school or home.

Comprehension Assessment

The questions in this section are modeled after current standardized tests to help students analyze what they've read and prepare for tests they may see in their classrooms. The questions are dependent on the text and require critical-thinking skills to answer.

Response to Literature

The final post-reading activity is an essay based on the text that also requires further research by students. This is a great way to extend this book into other curricular areas. A suggested rubric is provided for teacher reference.

Correlation to the Standards

Shell Education is committed to producing educational materials that are research and standards based. As part of this effort, we have correlated all of our products to the academic standards of all 50 states, the District of Columbia, the Department of Defense Dependents Schools, and all Canadian provinces.

Purpose and Intent of Standards

The Every Student Succeeds Act (ESSA) mandates that all states adopt challenging academic standards that help students meet the goal of college and career readiness. While many states already adopted academic standards prior to ESSA, the act continues to hold states accountable for detailed and comprehensive standards. Standards are statements that describe the criteria necessary for students to meet specific academic goals. They define the knowledge, skills, and content students should acquire at each level. State standards are used in the development of our products, so educators can be assured they meet state academic requirements.

How to Find Standards Correlations

To print a customized correlation report of this product for your state, visit our website at **www.teachercreatedmaterials.com/administrators/correlations/** and follow the online directions. If you require assistance in printing correlation reports, please contact our Customer Service Department at 1-877-777-3450.

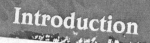
Correlation to the Standards (cont.)

Standards Correlation Chart

The lessons in this guide were written to support today's college and career readiness standards. This chart indicates which sections of this guide address which standards.

College and Career Readiness Standards	Section
Read closely to determine what the text says explicitly and to make logical inferences from it; cite specific textual evidence when writing or speaking to support conclusions drawn from the text.	Analyzing the Literature Sections 1–5; Close Reading the Literature Sections 1–5; Making Connections Sections 2–3; Creating with the Story Elements Sections 1–2, 4–5; Post-Reading Response to Literature
Determine central ideas or themes of a text and analyze their development; summarize the key supporting details and ideas.	Analyzing the Literature Sections 1–5; Making Connections Sections 2–3; Reader Response Sections 1–5; Culminating Activity
Analyze how and why individuals, events, or ideas develop and interact over the course of a text.	Analyzing the Literature Sections 1–5; Making Connections Section 3; Creating with the Story Elements Sections 1–3
Interpret words and phrases as they are used in a text, including determining technical, connotative, and figurative meanings, and analyze how specific word choices shape meaning or tone.	Vocabulary Sections 1–5; Making Connections Sections 3–4; Culminating Activity
Analyze the structure of texts, including how specific sentences, paragraphs, and larger portions of the text (e.g., a section, chapter, scene, or stanza) relate to each other and the whole.	Culminating Activity
Assess how point of view or purpose shapes the content and style of a text.	Making Connections Section 3; Creating with the Story Elements Sections 1, 3–4
Read and comprehend complex literary and informational texts independently and proficiently.	Entire Unit
Write arguments to support claims in an analysis of substantive topics or texts using valid reasoning and relevant and sufficient evidence.	Analyzing the Literature Sections 1–5; Reader Response Sections 1–4; Close Reading the Literature Sections 1–5; Culminating Activity
Write informative/explanatory texts to examine and convey complex ideas and information clearly and accurately through the effective selection, organization, and analysis of content.	Reader Response Sections 1, 5; Culminating Activity; Post-Reading Response to Literature
Write narratives to develop real or imagined experiences or events using effective technique, well-chosen details and well-structured event sequences.	Reader Response Sections 2–5; Making Connections Section 5; Creating with the Story Elements Sections 1–5

Introduction

Correlation to the Standards (cont.)

Standards Correlation Chart (cont.)

College and Career Readiness Standards	Section
Produce clear and coherent writing in which the development, organization, and style are appropriate to task, purpose, and audience.	Reader Response Sections 1–5; Making Connections Sections 4–5; Culminating Activity; Post-Reading Response to Literature
Develop and strengthen writing as needed by planning revisiting, editing, rewriting, or trying a new approach.	Culminating Activity; Post-Reading Response to Literature
Present information, findings, and supporting evidence such that listeners can follow the line of reasoning and the organization, development, and style are appropriate to task, purpose, and audience.	Culminating Activity
Demonstrate command of the conventions of standard English grammar and usage when writing or speaking.	Entire Unit
Demonstrate command of the conventions of standard English capitalization, punctuation, and spelling when writing.	Entire Unit
Determine or clarify the meaning of unknown and multiple-meaning words and phrases by using context clues, analyzing meaningful word parts, and consulting general and specialized reference materials, as appropriate.	Vocabulary Sections 1–5; Making Connections Section 4
Demonstrate understanding of figurative language, word relationships, and nuances in word meanings.	Making Connections Section 2
Acquire and use accurately a range of general academic and domain-specific words and phrases sufficient for reading, writing, speaking, and listening at the college and career readiness level; demonstrate independence in gathering vocabulary knowledge when encountering an unknown term important to comprehension or expression.	Vocabulary Sections 1–5

TESOL and WIDA Standards

The lessons in this book promote English language development for English language learners. The following TESOL and WIDA English Language Development Standards are addressed through the activities in this book:

- Standard 1: English language learners communicate for social and instructional purposes within the school setting.

- Standard 2: English language learners communicate information, ideas and concepts necessary for academic success in the content area of language arts.

About the Author—Kwame Alexander

Kwame Alexander was born in 1968 in New York City. At the time, his father was a graduate student at Bank Street Teacher's College, where one day he would return as a professor. He was also studying to become a Baptist minister. Kwame's mother was getting her master's degree in business education at Columbia University. She became a teacher, principal, and storyteller. She could hold a classroom of children in rapture over an African American folktale, playing all the characters, every one of them coming alive through the sound of her voice.

At the family home, she read poetry to Kwame and his sisters. She sang songs to them and told stories. Kwame loved his family, and he loved words and books. For him, there was almost no separation between family and literature.

He has authored over 21 books and is the recipient of many acclaimed awards, including the John Newbery Medal, the Coretta Scott King Award, the NCTE Charlotte Huck Award for Outstanding Fiction for Children, and the Paterson Poetry Prize to name a few. *The Crossover* has catapulted him into the spotlight, not only as an acclaimed fiction author but also as a poet and as a literary activist.

On April 5, 2016, Alexander described the change in his life since the publication of *The Crossover*, "I was on a jet plane on a runway. [With the Newbery call,] the plane took off. I've been soaring ever since."

Possible Texts for Text Comparisons

Other young adults books authored by Kwame Alexander could be used as enriching text comparisons. Titles include the following: *Booked*, *Crush*, and *He Said, She Said*.

Book Summary of *The Crossover*

Twin brothers, Josh and Jordan Bell, speed through life like they're always on a basketball court. Each twin has his own flare and style. Josh, also known as Filthy McNasty, prides himself on his wicked basketball skills, and he believes his long locks of hair are his wings, giving him the gift of flight on the court. He's the only one who can dunk on his team. Jordan, or JB, is obsessed with Michael Jordan and mirrors Jordan's on-the-court skill, short hair, and wardrobe. Being the stars of their school team, the twins seem to be in sync, both on and off the court. They sometimes know what each other wants before the other says it. Their loving parents cheer them on with zeal and pride on the court and at home.

Then, one day, things start to change. JB meets a girl he's interested in, and Josh starts to feel left out for the first time in his life. The two boys start to drift apart. More concerned with girls than basketball, JB seems always to be caught in a daydream. Josh, on the other hand, would like everything to remain the same. With growing boys comes growing drama.

In the background, their dad, Chuck Bell, is dealing with his own secret. Who will Josh turn to for life advice? Can everything get back to normal? Unlike basketball, there are no timeouts in life. Will the boys be able to reignite their groove on the court, or will issues off the court throw them off their game?

Cross-Curricular Connection

This novel can be used in a social studies unit on cultural geography and relationships. It ties into the literature themes of love, loss, family, friendships, and coming of age. It can also be used during a poetry unit focused on prose/verse structure and its impact on the tone or message of a story.

Possible Texts for Text Sets

- Applegate, Katherine. 2008. *Home of the Brave.* New York: Square Fish.
- Burg, Ann. 2012. *All the Broken Pieces.* New York: Scholastic.
- Creech, Sharon. 2001. *Love That Dog.* New York: HarperCollins.
- Grimes, Nikki. 2003. *Bronx Masquerade.* New York: Speak.
- Hesse, Karen. 2009. *Out of the Dust.* Wilmington: Great Source.
- Lai, Thanhha. 2013. *Inside Out & Back Again.* New York: HarperCollins.
- Smith, Hope Anita. 2011. *The Way a Door Closes.* New York: Square Fish.
- Woodson, Jacqueline. 2014. *Brown Girl Dreaming.* New York: Nancy Paulsen Books.

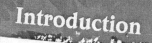
Name _____

Date _____

Pre-Reading Theme Thoughts

Directions: Read each of the statements. Decide if you agree or disagree with the statements. Record your opinion by marking an X in Agree or Disagree for each statement. Explain your choices in the fourth column. There are no right or wrong answers.

Statement	Agree	Disagree	Explain Your Answer
Children should not be forced to make hard decisions.			
When hard times come, you should always turn to your family.			
Sports are just like life, and you are the most-valuable player.			
If you don't have the support of your family, you don't have anything.			

Teacher Plans

Vocabulary Overview

Ten key words from this section are provided below with definitions and sentences about how the words are used in the book. Choose one of the vocabulary activity sheets (pages 15 or 16) for students to complete as they read this section. Monitor students as they work to ensure the definitions they have found are accurate and relate to the text. Finally, discuss these important vocabulary words with students. If you think these words or other words in the section warrant more time devoted to them, there are suggestions in the introduction for other vocabulary activities (page 5).

Word	Definition	Sentence about Text
acclaimed (pg. 4)	praised highly	Josh believes his game is so great it is **acclaimed**.
inspire (pg. 5)	influence	Josh thinks he can **inspire** anyone with his basketball skills.
dedicating (pg. 7)	naming something to honor someone	Dad **dedicates** the song "Filthy McNasty" to Josh, and just like that, Josh has a nickname.
agitating (pg. 10)	angering someone	Josh moves left, right, and then further right, **agitating** and confusing his opponents on the court.
elevating (pg. 10)	rising up	Josh thinks his locks are his basketball wings, **elevating** him higher and higher so he can dunk.
insists (pg. 11)	strongly states an opinion	JB **insists** that he does not idolize Michael Jordan, but he collects Air Jordan sneakers, and his room is covered in Jordan paraphernalia.
evidence (pg. 11)	something that proves the truth	JB wants to make all of his claims believable, so he supports them with **evidence**.
stalking (pg. 12)	watching and following closely	Josh jokes that JB is **stalking** Michael Jordan because he tries to copy everything he does.
banished (pg. 13)	sent away	The twins are **banished** to the backseat of the car when their parents ride in the front.
confrontational (pg. 16)	a situation when people oppose each other in anger	Dr. Bell says men who are too **confrontational** end up in jail.

Understanding Vocabulary Words

Directions: The following words appear in this section of the book. Use context clues and reference materials to determine an accurate definition for each word.

Word	Definition
acclaimed (pg. 4)	
inspire (pg. 5)	
dedicating (pg. 7)	
agitating (pg. 10)	
elevating (pg. 10)	
insists (pg. 11)	
evidence (pg. 11)	
stalking (pg. 12)	
banished (pg. 13)	
confrontational (pg. 16)	

Name _____

Date _____

During-Reading Vocabulary Activity

Directions: As you read these chapters, record at least eight important words on the lines below. Try to find interesting, difficult, intriguing, special, or funny words. Your words can be long or short. They can be hard or easy to spell. After each word, use context clues in the text and reference materials to define the word.

- _____
- _____
- _____
- _____
- _____
- _____
- _____
- _____
- _____

Directions: Respond to these questions about the words in this section.

1. Use details from "Warm-Up" to describe one way that Jordan **agitates** Josh.

   _____

   _____

2. Based on **evidence** from the story, what are two ways that Jordan has been **inspired** by Michael Jordan?

   _____

   _____

Analyzing the Literature

Provided below are discussion questions you can use in small groups, with the whole class, or for written assignments. Each question is given at two levels so you can choose the right question for each group of students. Activity sheets with these questions are provided (pages 18–19) if you want students to write their responses. For each question, a few key discussion points are provided for your reference.

Story Element	■ Level 1	▲ Level 2	Key Discussion Points
Character	Describe the twins and their family.	How are Josh and Jordan Bell similar? How are they different?	Jordan and Josh both play basketball for their school team. Josh plays the forward position and has long dreadlocks. Jordan, also called JB, is a guard and keeps his hair cut short. Jordan is a huge Michal Jordan fan and likes to bet on just about anything. Josh mostly focuses on basketball.
Plot	Why does Chuck Bell nickname Josh *Filthy McNasty*?	What do you learn about Josh and his father based on the day Chuck nicknames Josh?	Josh and his dad are listening to jazz music together, and Horace Silver's song "Filthy McNasty" comes on. Chuck dedicates the song to his son because it's the "best song, the funkiest song" on the album. This scene illustrates how the father and son use humor and common interests to communicate and get along.
Character	Describe the relationship between Josh and his father.	How can you tell that Josh admires his father?	Josh and his father have a loving relationship. They joke around a lot and spend time together. While Josh thinks that some of the things his father does are outdated, he likes being around his dad and hearing his jokes.
Setting	How are the poems about basketball different from the other poems in the first section?	Why did Kwame Alexander write "Dribbling" the way he did? What connections can be made between the setting and the poem's structure?	The poem "Dribbling" is written to elicit movement and describe what is happening on the court in the middle of a basketball game. During a game, movement is swift and rapid and Alexander captures this movement by writing the poem visually.

Name _____

Date _____

Analyzing the Literature

Directions: Think about the section you just read. Read each question and state your response with textual evidence.

1. Describe the twins and their family.

   _____

   _____

   _____

   _____

2. Why does Chuck Bell nickname Josh *Filthy McNasty*?

   _____

   _____

   _____

   _____

3. Describe the relationship between Josh and his father.

   _____

   _____

   _____

   _____

4. How are the poems about basketball different from the other poems in the first section?

   _____

   _____

   _____

   _____

Name _____

Date _____

▲ Analyzing the Literature

Directions: Think about the section you just read. Read each question and state your response with textual evidence.

1. How are Josh and Jordan Bell similar? How are they different?

   _____

   _____

   _____

   _____

2. What do you learn about Josh and his father based on the day Chuck nicknames Josh?

   _____

   _____

   _____

   _____

3. How can you tell that Josh admires his father?

   _____

   _____

   _____

   _____

4. Why did Kwame Alexander write "Dribbling" the way he did? What connections can be made between the setting and the poem's structure?

   _____

   _____

   _____

Name _____

Date _____

Reader Response

Directions: Choose one of the following prompts about this section to answer. Be sure you include a topic sentence in your response, use textual evidence to support your opinion, and provide a strong conclusion that summarizes your opinion.

Writing Prompts

- **Informative/Explanatory Piece**—When someone gives a person a nickname, it is usually seen as a badge of honor. In what ways are nicknames important? In what ways can they be negative?
- **Opinion/Argument Piece**—The poem, "Basketball Rule #1," on page 20 describes how Chuck Bell feels about basketball. Explain the reasons why you do or do not agree with this point of view.

_____

_____

_____

_____

_____

_____

_____

_____

_____

_____

_____

_____

Name _____

Date _____

Close Reading the Literature

Directions: Closely reread pages 8–10 when Josh describes how he feels about his nickname. Read each question below and revisit the text to find evidence to support your answers.

1. Based on the text, how does Josh feel about his nickname at first?

    _____

    _____

    _____

2. What happened to change Josh's opinion about his nickname?

    _____

    _____

    _____

3. What does the text tell you about how Josh feels about his father?

    _____

    _____

    _____

    _____

4. How do the unique words, such as "combinating," "UNCOOLed," and "dunkalicious," on page 10 make the "Filthy McNasty" poem stand out from the rest of the book?

    _____

    _____

    _____

    _____

Name _____

Date _____

Making Connections–The Nickname Game

Kwame Alexander opens the book by introducing the twins and how they received their nicknames. Getting a nickname, especially if you receive one from someone you admire, is usually a proud moment. Do you have a nickname? How did you get the nickname? Do you want a nickname or a different nickname?

Directions: Use the comic strip below to sequence how you received your nickname, or if you don't have a nickname, sketch a scenario where you might receive a nickname. Be sure to include words, images, and other sketches to make your comic strip engaging.

Name _____

Date _____

Creating with the Story Elements

Directions: Thinking about the story elements of character, setting, and plot in a novel is very important to understanding what is happening and why. Complete **one** of the following activities based on what you've read so far. Be creative and have fun!

Characters

Josh loves his locked hair. Write a rhyme, poem, or rap pretending you are Josh explaining how much your locks mean to you.

Setting

Based on what you know about Jordan and Josh, create a sketch of how their rooms might look. Make sure to include their likes, interests, and hobbies.

Plot

Think about the types of lessons that Jordan and Josh receive from their parents. How might an ex-professional athlete and an assistant school principal relate differently to the twins? Create a Venn diagram to show the differences between how the parents treat their children.

Vocabulary Overview

Ten key words from this section are provided below with definitions and sentences about how the words are used in the book. Choose one of the vocabulary activity sheets (pages 25 or 26) for students to complete as they read this section. Monitor students as they work to ensure the definitions they have found are accurate and relate to the text. Finally, discuss these important vocabulary words with students. If you think these words or other words in the section warrant more time devoted to them, there are suggestions in the introduction for other vocabulary activities (page 5).

Word	Definition	Sentence about Text
phenomenal (pg. 23)	outstanding, remarkable	The twins are the most **phenomenal** players on the school's basketball team.
impersonation (pg. 25)	imitation of someone else	The coach does an **impersonation** of Phil Jackson, who is a famous basketball coach.
taunt (pg. 26)	to challenge someone with insults	On the court, Jordan **taunts** the opposing team.
enshrine (pg. 33)	to protect something valuable	Josh is so attached to his hair that, if he could, he would **enshrine** it and preserve it forever.
cackles (pg. 37)	laughs loudly or harshly	When Jordan wins the bet, he **cackles** loudly as he approaches Josh with the scissors.
seldom (pg. 43)	rarely	It is **seldom** that Josh uses math outside of school; however, when Jordan cuts his locks off, he sadly counts them.
rummaging (pg. 45)	actively searching for something	The twins cannot resist **rummaging** through their dad's basketball memorabilia.
pivot (pg. 51)	to turn around in one spot	Chuck Bell teaches his sons the fundamentals of basketball: to move swiftly, **pivot** when double-teamed, and stay in control of the ball.
camaraderie (pg. 80)	a feeling of friendship	Once Jordan starts to date Miss Sweet Tea, Alexis, the brothers start to lose their sense of **camaraderie**.
imbecile (pg. 80)	an idiotic person	Josh thinks Jordan is acting like an **imbecile** about Alexis.

Name _____

Date _____

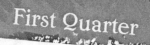

Understanding Vocabulary Words

Directions: The following words appear in this section of the book. Use context clues and reference materials to determine an accurate definition for each word.

Word	Definition
phenomenal (pg. 23)	
impersonation (pg. 25)	
taunt (pg. 26)	
enshrine (pg. 33)	
cackles (pg. 37)	
seldom (pg. 43)	
rummaging (pg. 45)	
pivot (pg. 51)	
camaraderie (pg. 80)	
imbecile (pg. 80)	

Name _____

Date _____

During-Reading Vocabulary Activity

Directions: As you read these chapters, record at least eight important words on the lines below. Try to find interesting, difficult, intriguing, special, or funny words. Your words can be long or short. They can be hard or easy to spell. After each word, use context clues in the text and reference materials to define the word.

- _____
- _____
- _____
- _____
- _____
- _____
- _____
- _____
- _____
- _____

Directions: Respond to these questions about the words in this section.

1. In what ways does JB **taunt** the players from other teams?

   _____

   _____

2. Why do the twins **rummage** through their dad's things?

   _____

   _____

Analyzing the Literature

Provided below are discussion questions you can use in small groups, with the whole class, or for written assignments. Each question is given at two levels so you can choose the right question for each group of students. Activity sheets with these questions are provided (pages 28–29) if you want students to write their responses. For each question, a few key discussion points are provided for your reference.

Story Element	■ Level 1	▲ Level 2	Key Discussion Points
Character	Describe Chuck and Dr. Bell.	How might you describe the relationship between the twins and their parents?	Chuck and Dr. Bell are Josh and Jordan's parents. Both parents clearly love and care for the boys, but Chuck likes to joke where Dr. Bell is considered the sterner parent.
Plot	Why did JB give up extra summer basketball practice to go to Sunday school, and what does Josh think about this?	How might JB choosing girls over basketball be foreshadowing for something else to come? What do you think this means for the boys' relationship?	This is the first time in the book (and maybe their lives) where the boys have a very different opinion on things. Usually, they are very focused on basketball. Recently, though, JB has taken an interest in girls and has put basketball aside. This might cause a rift between the boys since Josh thinks focusing on girls over basketball is crazy!
Character	How do Chuck and Dr. Bell differ in their eating habits?	Why do you think Dr. Bell is concerned about what the family eats?	Chuck Bell is prone to hypertension and had to leave professional basketball because of a muscle condition. Dr. Bell is worried that he is not taking care of himself, and they argue about this matter a lot. Chuck often sneaks off to eat unhealthy food with the twins, and Dr. Bell tries to balance that out by monitoring what they eat together.
Plot	Who is the new girl?	How do the boys react to the new girl?	There is a new girl at the school. She is initially described only by what she is wearing (tight jeans and pink sneakers). Both boys are instantly interested in her—JB outwardly and Josh secretly. She initially talks to Josh, but then comes to the basketball game with a drink for JB.

Name _____

Date _____

Analyzing the Literature

Directions: Think about the section you just read. Read each question and state your response with textual evidence.

1. Describe Chuck and Dr. Bell.

_____

_____

_____

_____

2. Why did JB give up extra summer basketball practice to go to Sunday school, and what does Josh think about this?

_____

_____

_____

_____

3. How do Chuck and Dr. Bell differ in their eating habits?

_____

_____

_____

_____

4. Who is the new girl?

_____

_____

_____

_____

Name _____

Date _____

▲ Analyzing the Literature

Directions: Think about the section you just read. Read each question and state your response with textual evidence.

1. How might you describe the relationship between the twins and their parents?

_____

_____

_____

_____

2. How might JB choosing girls over basketball be foreshadowing for something else to come? What do you think this means for the boys' relationship?

_____

_____

_____

_____

3. Why do you think Dr. Bell is concerned about what the family eats?

_____

_____

_____

4. How do the boys react to the new girl?

_____

_____

_____

Name _____

Date _____

Reader Response

Directions: Choose one of the following prompts about this section to answer. Be sure you include a topic sentence in your response, use textual evidence to support your opinion, and provide a strong conclusion that summarizes your opinion.

Writing Prompts

- **Narrative Piece**—The situation for Josh seems to be spiraling out of his control. He feels that he is losing his brother and can't do anything about it. Write a narrative poem that tells Josh how he can ensure that he and his brother stay close. Give him some advice!

- **Opinion/Argument Piece**—There are many things going through Josh's head at this point in the book. Based on the text, what are the most important of his concerns?

_____

_____

_____

_____

_____

_____

_____

_____

_____

_____

_____

_____

Close Reading the Literature

Directions: Closely reread "The inside of Mom and Dad's bedroom closet" on pages 44–47. Read each question and then revisit the text to find evidence that supports your answer.

1. For what reasons do JB and Josh like to look through their parents' closet?

   _____

   _____

   _____

   _____

2. Based on this scene, how does JB feel about the fact that he cut Josh's hair?

   _____

   _____

   _____

   _____

3. How do you know that they are excited about finding their father's championship ring?

   _____

   _____

   _____

4. From what you know about Chuck Bell, why might he have decided "not to have surgery" even though it ended his career?

   _____

   _____

   _____

Name _____

Date _____

Making Connections—Life Rules

Directions: Chuck Bell writes Basketball Rules for his sons. Each one relates life on the court to everyday life and has a double meaning. There have been four rules in the book so far. Reread those poems. Then, think about life and basketball, and write your own rule. Draw a picture to support your rule.

Basketball Rule #____

_____

_____

_____

_____

_____

_____

_____

_____

_____

_____

_____

_____

_____

_____

Name _____

Date _____

Creating with the Story Elements

Directions: Thinking about the story elements of character, setting, and plot in a novel is very important to understanding what is happening and why. Complete **one** of the following activities based on what you've read so far. Be creative and have fun!

Characters

Make up clever nicknames for Vondie, Dr. Bell, and the coach. Explain why you gave them these names.

Setting

In "Gym class," Josh has many thoughts running through his head. Sketch Josh and draw 3–4 thought bubbles to illustrate some of the things he is thinking about.

Plot

When the new girl walks up to Josh at the end of the game, he thinks she is there to see him. Pretend you are Josh, and write a poem about how you feel at the moment you realize she is waiting for your brother.

Vocabulary Overview

Ten key words from this section are provided below with definitions and sentences about how the words are used in the book. Choose one of the vocabulary activity sheets (pages 35 or 36) for students to complete as they read this section. Monitor students as they work to ensure the definitions they have found are accurate and relate to the text. Finally, discuss these important vocabulary words with students. If you think these words or other words in the section warrant more time devoted to them, there are suggestions in the introduction for other vocabulary activities (page 5).

Word	Definition	Sentence about Text
struts (pg. 94)	walks proudly	After a win, the twins **strut** off the court into the locker room.
violation (pg. 95)	an action that is against the rules	The referee calls a moving **violation** on JB during the game.
stroke (pg. 97)	an illness where blood vessels in the brain break	The twins' grandfather had a **stroke**.
curious (pg. 104)	wanting and eager to learn more	Josh is **curious** about Jordan's girlfriend.
humorous (pg. 104)	funny	Irony can sometimes be **humorous**.
opulent (pg. 107)	very wealthy, rich	The Bells are not **opulent**, but they have enough money to be comfortable.
reputation (pg. 107)	how you are perceived by others	Jordan thinks that showing students at school that he is smart will ruin his **reputation**.
verdict (pg. 108)	the end decision or result	The **verdict** is in … Jordan and Alexis are officially boyfriend and girlfriend.
superior (pg. 110)	higher quality than the rest	According to JB, Michael Jordan is **superior** to all other basketball players.
stubble (pg. 120)	very short hair just growing in	Josh has itching **stubble** on his head after he shaves off his hair.

Name _____

Date _____

Understanding Vocabulary Words

Directions: The following words appear in this section of the book. Use context clues and reference materials to determine an accurate definition for each word.

Word	Definition
struts (pg. 94)	
violation (pg. 95)	
stroke (pg. 97)	
curious (pg. 104)	
humorous (pg. 104)	
opulent (pg. 107)	
reputation (pg. 107)	
verdict (pg. 108)	
superior (pg. 110)	
stubble (pg. 120)	

Name _____

Date _____

During-Reading Vocabulary Activity

Directions: As you read these chapters, record at least eight important words on the lines below. Try to find interesting, difficult, intriguing, special, or funny words. Your words can be long or short. They can be hard or easy to spell. After each word, use context clues in the text and reference materials to define the word.

- _____

- _____

- _____

- _____

- _____

- _____

- _____

- _____

- _____

- _____

Directions: Now, organize your words. Rewrite each of your words on a sticky note. Work as a group to create a bar graph of your words. You should stack any words that are the same on top of one another. Different words appear in different columns. Finally, discuss with a group why certain words were chosen more often than other words.

Analyzing the Literature

Provided below are discussion questions you can use in small groups, with the whole class, or for written assignments. Each question is given at two levels so you can choose the right question for each group of students. Activity sheets with these questions are provided (pages 38–39) if you want students to write their responses. For each question, a few key discussion points are provided for your reference.

Story Element	■ Level 1	▲ Level 2	Key Discussion Points
Character	How does Josh describe the changes in his brother to his father?	What does Josh feel about how JB is acting now that he's interested in Alexis?	Josh complains to his father that Jordan is acting strangely. He notes that Jordan is always smiling, getting spacey, wearing cologne, and texting Alexis. Josh begs his father to help him get Jordan back to normal.
Plot	Why is Dr. Bell trying to get the family to eat differently?	For what reasons does Dr. Bell have concerns about her family's eating habits?	Dr. Bell knows that Chuck should go to the doctor to be checked out, and this point is the main cause of conflict between the parents. Chuck's father had a stroke, and Chuck has recently had a few issues with his health in front of the boys. She has valid cause for her concern.
Character	How has the twins' relationship changed since the beginning of the book?	What do you think is causing the twins' relationship to change?	Most of the tension arises from Jordan's girlfriend, Alexis, but some of it is because Josh feels abandoned by his brother. Earlier in the book, it states that Jordan skipped summer basketball camp to spend time with a girl. So the change has been coming for a while now.
Plot	What happens between JB and Jordan during the game at the end of the section?	What incidents lead up to Josh's explosion at the end of this section?	Josh finally hits his tipping point during the middle of the game. The stress of JB's relationship, being late to the game, and getting caught up in the moment are too much for Josh. He explodes and fires the ball right at his brother's face.

Name _____

Date _____

■ Analyzing the Literature

Directions: Think about the section you just read. Read each question and state your response with textual evidence.

1. How does Josh describe the changes in his brother to his father?

_____

_____

_____

_____

2. Why is Dr. Bell trying to get the family to eat differently?

_____

_____

_____

_____

3. How has the twins' relationship changed since the beginning of the book?

_____

_____

_____

_____

4. What happens between JB and Jordan during the game at the end of the section?

_____

_____

_____

_____

▲ Analyzing the Literature

Directions: Think about the section you just read. Read each question and state your response with textual evidence.

1. What does Josh feel about how JB is acting now that he's interested in Alexis?

    _____

    _____

    _____

    _____

2. For what reasons does Dr. Bell have concerns about her family's eating habits?

    _____

    _____

    _____

    _____

3. What do you think is causing the twins' relationship to change?

    _____

    _____

    _____

    _____

4. What incidents lead up to Josh's explosion at the end of this section?

    _____

    _____

    _____

    _____

Name _____

Date _____

Reader Response

Directions: Choose one of the following prompts about this section to answer. Be sure you include a topic sentence in your response, use textual evidence to support your opinion, and provide a strong conclusion that summarizes your opinion.

Writing Prompts

- **Opinion/Argument Piece**—Discuss the issues that brought Josh to his tipping point during this section of the book. How might you have reacted if put in the same position?
- **Narrative Piece**—Write a biography of Chuck Bell based on what you know about him so far.

_____

_____

_____

_____

_____

_____

_____

_____

_____

_____

_____

_____

_____

Name _____

Date _____

Close Reading the Literature

Directions: Closely reread pages 89–94 at the beginning of the Second Quarter. Read each question, and then revisit the text to find evidence that supports your answer.

1. On page 91, Chuck Bell says, "talking to your brother right now would be like pushing water uphill with a rake." What does he mean by this?

_____

_____

_____

_____

2. How does "Basketball Rule #5" relate to what has happened in the book so far?

_____

_____

_____

3. What does Josh mean when he says, "Dad, this girl is making / Jordan act weird. / He's here, but he's not."

_____

_____

_____

4. Describe at least two ways that the layout of the text on page 94 makes "Showoff" more interesting than some of the other poems?

_____

_____

_____

Name _____

Date _____

Making Connections—Describe the Ways

Directions: Poets use verse to express their feelings and explain their thoughts. Josh reaches his "tipping point" during the middle of a basketball game. Write an ode, acrostic, ballad, rap, or other poem that responds to one of the following:

- How does Josh feel right before he throws the ball at Jordan?

- How does Jordan feel emotionally in the moments after the ball hits him?

_____

_____

_____

_____

_____

_____

_____

_____

_____

_____

_____

_____

_____

_____

Name _____

Date _____

Creating with the Story Elements

Directions: Thinking about the story elements of character, setting, and plot in a novel is very important to understanding what is happening and why. Complete **one** of the following activities based on what you've read so far. Be creative and have fun!

Characters

Create a Venn diagram for Josh. On one side, list all of the positive qualities of his personality. On the other side, list the negative qualities of his personality. In the middle, include attributes that both help and hurt the other characters in the story.

Setting

At this point, the book has taken place in several locations. Draw a map of the Bells' community. Make sure to include the school, their house, the restaurants they visit, the recreation center, the library, and other places important to the plot of the novel.

Plot

The story is told from Josh's point of view. Write a description of how the story would be different if it were told from JB's point of view.

Teacher Plans

Vocabulary Overview

Ten key words from this section are provided below with definitions and sentences about how the words are used in the book. Choose one of the vocabulary activity sheets (pages 45 or 46) for students to complete as they read this section. Monitor students as they work to ensure the definitions they have found are accurate and relate to the text. Finally, discuss these important vocabulary words with the students. If you think these words or other words in the section warrant more time devoted to them, there are suggestions in the introduction for other vocabulary activities (page 5).

Word	Definition	Sentence about Text
volcanic (pg. 137)	extremely angry	After Josh bloodies JB's nose, the unspoken words from his parents are **volcanic**.
churlish (pg. 138)	not polite; rude	Josh acts **churlishly** when he throws the ball at his brother.
deranged (pg. 139)	insane	Dr. Bell tells Josh that he has been **deranged** for the past few weeks.
discipline (pg. 140)	control gained by following rules and punishment for bad behavior	Josh's mother believes that "Boys with no **discipline** end up in prison."
flagrant (pg. 151)	bad enough that it can't be ignored	When the referee doesn't call the **flagrant** foul, Chuck storms to the court.
remarkable (pg. 155)	noticeably extraordinary	The Wildcats have a **remarkable** season and are heading to the championship.
phenom (pg. 155)	someone who excels at something	Josh and JB are basketball **phenoms**.
eavesdropping (pg. 173)	sneakily listening in on someone's conversation	When his parents talk about health-related issues, Josh **eavesdrops**.
distractions (pg. 186)	things that make it hard to concentrate, focus, or think	The coach tells Josh to get a handle on his **distractions** and get his head back in the game.
interruption (pg. 187)	something that is stopped from happening for awhile	The feud with JB causes an **interruption** in the twin's relationship.

Name _____

Date _____

Understanding Vocabulary Words

Directions: The following words appear in this section of the book. Use context clues and reference materials to determine an accurate definition for each word.

Word	Definition
volcanic (pg. 137)	
churlish (pg. 138)	
deranged (pg. 139)	
discipline (pg. 140)	
flagrant (pg. 151)	
remarkable (pg. 155)	
phenom (pg. 155)	
eavesdropping (pg. 173)	
distractions (pg. 186)	
interruption (pg. 187)	

Name _____

Date _____

During-Reading Vocabulary Activity

Directions: As you read these chapters, record at least eight important words on the lines below. Try to find interesting, difficult, intriguing, special, or funny words. Your words can be long or short. They can be hard or easy to spell. After each word, use context clues in the text and reference materials to define the word.

- _____

- _____

- _____

- _____

- _____

- _____

- _____

- _____

- _____

Directions: Respond to these questions about the words in this section.

1. How is Josh **disciplined** after he injures JB?

   _____

   _____

2. What **distractions** have been occupying Josh's mind lately?

   _____

   _____

Analyzing the Literature

Provided below are discussion questions you can use in small groups, with the whole class, or for written assignments. Each question is given at two levels so you can choose the right question for each group of students. Activity sheets with these questions are provided (pages 48–49) if you want students to write their responses. For each question, a few key discussion points are provided for your reference.

Story Element	■ Level 1	▲ Level 2	Key Discussion Points
Plot	What are the indicators that Chuck has serious health issues?	Chuck is clearly ill, why doesn't he go to the doctor now?	Chuck doesn't like going to the doctor because his father went for a check up and died in the hospital. These spells (nose bleed, vomiting, etc.) are probably not good indications of his health.
Plot	Tension is rising between Chuck and Dr. Bell. What is causing this tension?	What are some ways Chuck and Dr. Bell could fix the issues they have been arguing about?	Things between Chuck and Dr. Bell are tense because Chuck is sick and refuses to go to the doctor. Dr. Bell would like him to get a check up as well as cut back on unhealthy eating. She thinks these will help him be healthier.
Character	What do you think it will take for JB to forgive his brother?	For what reasons does Josh blame JB for their feud?	The twins are at an impasse, but with time JB should be able to forgive his brother. The brothers are at odds because Josh feels abandoned. He doesn't have a girlfriend, has no one to play basketball with, and his parents seem to be preoccupied. He feels alone and blames JB.
Character	Describe what we learn about Alexis in this section.	In what ways could learning more about Alexis help and/or harm the relationship between the brothers?	Alexis plays basketball at the Rec center. She follows the WNBA as well as the NBA. Her parents are divorced, and she lives with her father. Her sister goes to Duke. Learning about her might be helpful because Josh will see why JB likes her. It could be harmful because Josh might still feel he has been replaced.

Name _____

Date _____

Analyzing the Literature

Directions: Think about the section you just read. Read each question and state your response with textual evidence.

1. What are the indicators that Chuck has serious health issues?

_____

_____

_____

_____

2. Tension is rising between Chuck and Dr. Bell. What is causing this tension?

_____

_____

_____

_____

3. What do you think it will take for JB to forgive his brother?

_____

_____

_____

_____

4. Describe what we learn about Alexis in this section.

_____

_____

_____

_____

Name _____

Date _____

▲ Analyzing the Literature

Directions: Think about the section you just read. Read each question and state your response with textual evidence.

1. Chuck is clearly ill, why doesn't he go to the doctor now?

_____

_____

_____

_____

2. What are some ways Chuck and Dr. Bell could fix the issues they have been arguing about?

_____

_____

_____

_____

3. For what reasons does Josh blame JB for their feud?

_____

_____

_____

_____

4. In what ways could learning more about Alexis help and/or harm the relationship between the brothers?

_____

_____

_____

_____

Name _____

Date _____

Reader Response

Directions: Choose one of the following prompts about this section to answer. Be sure you include a topic sentence in your response, use textual evidence to support your opinion, and provide a strong conclusion that summarizes your opinion.

Writing Prompts

- **Opinion/Argument Piece**—Chuck Bell doesn't like to go to the doctor. Based on the text, should he heed his wife's advice and go to the doctor?
- **Narrative Piece**—Josh's actions cause a rift between him and Jordan. Have you ever been on the outs with a sibling or friend? Give Josh some advice to fix the problem and mend his relationship with Jordan.

_____

_____

_____

_____

_____

_____

_____

_____

_____

_____

_____

_____

_____

Close Reading the Literature

Directions: Closely reread pages 159–161 at the end of this section. Read each question and then revisit the text to find evidence that supports your answer.

1. Based on the text, why does Josh decide to write JB an apology letter?

   _____

   _____

   _____

   _____

2. In his apology letter to JB, to what does Josh compare their relationship?

   _____

   _____

   _____

3. Use the text to explain what Josh's analogies mean in relation to the brothers.

   _____

   _____

   _____

   _____

4. What makes Josh think that JB may have read his letter even if he's not reacting to it yet?

   _____

   _____

   _____

   _____

Name _____

Date _____

Making Connections–Vocabulary Focus

Directions: Throughout the book, Kwame Alexander pulls vocabulary words aside and gives definitions and examples. Look through the book and reread some of these pages. The first one is on page 29, and the most recent one is on page 187. Now, choose a word from the text that hasn't been defined yet. Create your own page that includes a definition and examples of the word using the characters, plot, and setting of *The Crossover*.

_____

_____

_____

_____

_____

_____

_____

_____

_____

_____

_____

_____

_____

Name _____

Date _____

Creating with the Story Elements

Directions: Thinking about the story elements of character, setting, and plot in a novel is very important to understanding what is happening and why. Complete **one** of the following activities based on what you've read so far. Be creative and have fun!

Characters

Create a cause-and-effect chart showing at least four events from the story that lead to Chuck Bell collapsing while playing basketball with Josh.

Setting

Make a poster explaining the importance of health and CPR training in school physical education classes. Add images and words to create a poster that has a strong impact on everyone who sees it.

Plot

Write a poem predicting what you think will happen to the Bell family next. How will the twins respond to the collapse of their father? How will Dr. Bell deal with what comes next?

Vocabulary Overview

Ten key words from this section are provided below with definitions and sentences about how the words are used in the book. Choose one of the vocabulary activity sheets (pages 55 or 56) for students to complete as they read this section. Monitor students as they work to ensure the definitions they have found are accurate and relate to the text. Finally, discuss these important vocabulary words with students. If you think these words or other words in the section warrant more time devoted to them, there are suggestions in the introduction for other vocabulary activities (page 5).

Word	Definition	Sentence about Text
stable (pg. 199)	in a good condition that may not change	The doctors say Chuck is **stable** enough to have visitors.
splintered (pg. 204)	pieces broken off from a larger structure	Josh is angry because their backboard is **splintered**.
possession (pg. 205)	owning something	When the team has **possession** of the ball, they make an attempt to score before the buzzer.
dedicated (pg. 205)	offered appreciation and loyalty	Because Chuck Bell is in the hospital, the team **dedicates** the game to him.
intention (pg. 208)	a plan to act in a certain way	It isn't Chuck Bell's **intention** to end up in the hospital.
Tanka (pg. 212)	a Japanese poem that follows a syllable count of 5/7/5/7/7	Josh is assigned to write a **Tanka** poem but can only think of his dad.
complications (pg. 218)	having difficult times	After being declared stable, Chuck starts to have **complications** while in the hospital.
quivering (pg. 221)	shuddering because of being scared	Josh tells himself to stop **quivering** as he drives to make the winning shot.
inevitable (pg. 230)	guaranteed to occur	"Basketball Rule #10" says that loss is **inevitable**.
wedge (pg. 234)	stuck between two things	The boys store their basketball **wedged** between the rim and the backboard.

Name _____

Date _____

Understanding Vocabulary Words

Directions: The following words appear in this section of the book. Use context clues and reference materials to determine an accurate definition for each word.

Word	Definition
stable (pg. 199)	
splintered (pg. 204)	
possession (pg. 205)	
dedicated (pg. 205)	
intention (pg. 208)	
Tanka (pg. 212)	
complications (pg. 218)	
quivering (pg. 221)	
inevitable (pg. 230)	
wedge (pg. 234)	

Name _____

Date _____

During-Reading Vocabulary Activity

Directions: As you read these chapters, choose five important words from the story. Then, use those five words to complete this word flow chart. On each arrow, write a vocabulary word. In the boxes between the words, explain how the words connect. An example for the words *stable* and *quivering* has been done for you.

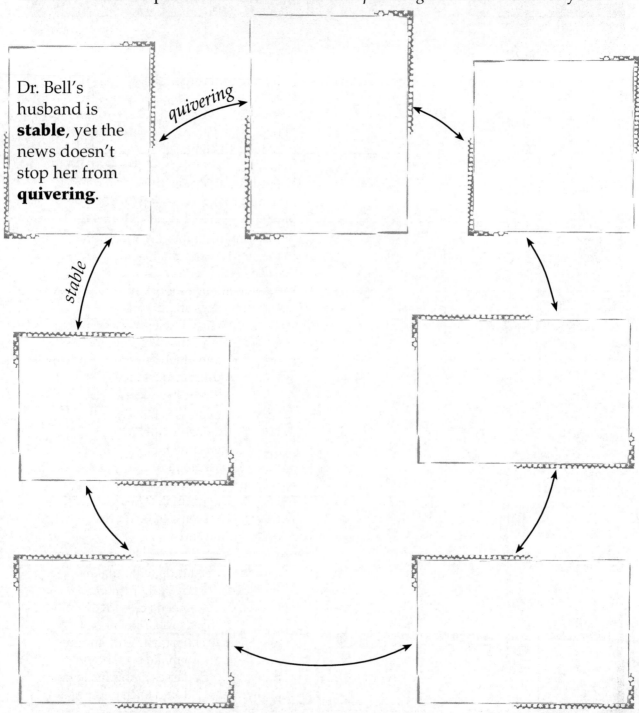

Dr. Bell's husband is **stable**, yet the news doesn't stop her from **quivering**.

quivering

stable

Analyzing the Literature

Provided below are discussion questions you can use in small groups, with the whole class, or for written assignments. Each question is given at two levels so you can choose the right question for each group of students. Activity sheets with these questions are provided (pages 58–59) if you want students to write their responses. For each question, a few key discussion points are provided for your reference.

Story Element	■ Level 1	▲ Level 2	Key Discussion Points
Character	Why is Josh initially upset to be at the hospital with his dad?	Describe Josh's feelings about being at the hospital with his dad. How do his feelings change during this time?	Josh would rather be at the game. He was suspended from the last few games, and now that he has been reinstated, he would rather be playing with his team than at the hospital with his dad. Most likely, his frustration is misdirected, and he is scared to be in the hospital.
Setting	What do Josh and his father discuss in the hospital?	How do you think the "question" conversation with his father affects Josh?	Josh and his father aren't sure what to say to one another, so they have a "question" conversation. In that conversation, a lot of important information is shared. Josh wants to know why Chuck didn't go to the doctor sooner and if he is going to die. The conversation ends with Josh still being hurt and confused.
Plot	How does each boy deal with the illness and death of his father?	How does Chuck's death affect the relationship between the twins?	Each boy expresses his fear and pain differently. Josh wants to pretend everything is fine and continues playing basketball to honor his father. Jordan goes to the hospital and can't keep acting normal. The death of their father seems to bring the boys closer in the end.
Character	Why does Chuck give his championship ring to Josh?	How do you think JB feels as he hands their dad's championship ring to Josh?	Chuck understands what makes each of his boys successful. Josh needs basketball. He needs crossovers and dunks. JB needs relationships. He needs his friends, girlfriend, mother, and brother. To make both boys happy, Chuck passes along his legacy knowing they'll find each other again.

Name _____

Date _____

Analyzing the Literature

Directions: Think about the section you just read. Read each question and state your response with textual evidence.

1. Why is Josh initially upset to be at the hospital with his dad?

_____

_____

_____

_____

2. What do Josh and his father discuss in the hospital?

_____

_____

_____

_____

3. How does each boy deal with the illness and death of his father?

_____

_____

_____

_____

4. Why does Chuck give his championship ring to Josh?

_____

_____

_____

_____

Name _____

Date _____

▲ Analyzing the Literature

Directions: Think about the section you just read. Read each question and state your response with textual evidence.

1. Describe Josh's feelings about being at the hospital with his dad. How do his feelings change during this time?

   _____

   _____

   _____

   _____

2. How do you think the "question" conversation with his father affects Josh?

   _____

   _____

   _____

   _____

3. How does Chuck's death affect the relationship between the twins?

   _____

   _____

   _____

   _____

4. How do you think JB feels as he hands their dad's championship ring to Josh?

   _____

   _____

   _____

Name _____

Date _____

Reader Response

Directions: Choose one of the following prompts about this section to answer. Be sure you include a topic sentence in your response, use textual evidence to support your opinion, and provide a strong conclusion that summarizes your opinion.

Writing Prompts

- **Informative/Explanatory Piece**—What are at least three unanswered questions that you have about the book? Describe why you included each question.
- **Narrative Piece**—Write an epilogue for the novel that is set five years in the future. Include information about the twins and Dr. Bell.

_____

_____

_____

_____

_____

_____

_____

_____

_____

_____

_____

_____

_____

Name _____

Date _____

Close Reading the Literature

Directions: Closely reread pages 215–222 at the end of this section. Read each question and then revisit the text to find evidence that supports your answer.

1. How does the author use figurative language on page 215?

    _____

    _____

    _____

    _____

2. Based on what you know about the characters, why do Josh and JB make different decisions about what to do on page 216?

    _____

    _____

    _____

    _____

3. The basketball game is a tight match, and as Coach calls a time-out, Josh thinks, "I wish the ref could stop the clock of my life." Use the text to explain why he has this thought.

    _____

    _____

    _____

4. Based on the text, what happens at the end of this section?

    _____

    _____

    _____

Name _____

Date _____

Making Connections—What If?

Directions: At the end of the book, Chuck Bell passes away. Think about how the novel would end differently if Chuck were alive. What if Chuck had gone to the doctor in the first section when we first learned about his wife's concerns? What if he'd had the knee surgery and continued to play professional basketball? What if he had gone to the doctor when he had the nosebleed or vomited in the house? How do you think the novel might have ended differently? Create an outline in the space below, and then write an alternate Overtime to the story.

_____

_____

_____

_____

_____

_____

_____

_____

_____

_____

_____

_____

_____

_____

_____

Name _____

Date _____

Creating with the Story Elements

Directions: Thinking about the story elements of character, setting, and plot in a novel is very important to understanding what is happening and why. Complete **one** of the following activities based on what you've read so far. Be creative and have fun!

Characters

Haiku are short poems of three lines. The syllable counts of each line are 5/7/5. Write a series of haiku poems as if you are one of the twins communicating with a friend about how you feel after your father's death.

Setting

Draw a picture that shows the final second during the championship game. Be sure to include the basket, the ball, Josh, JB, and Alexis in your image.

Plot

In this last section, Josh goes to the game and Jordan goes to the hospital to be with their father. How would the end of the book have changed if both boys had gone to the hospital or if both boys had gone to the game? Outline a new story detailing how the plot would have changed, where the story would have gone, and how would it have ended.

Name _____

Date _____

Post-Reading Theme Thoughts

Directions: Read each of the statements. Choose a main character from *The Crossover*. Think about that character's point of view. From that character's perspective, decide if the character would agree or disagree with the statements. Record the character's opinion by marking an X in Agree or Disagree for each statement. Explain your choices in the fourth column using text evidence.

Character I Chose: _____

Statement	Agree	Disagree	Explain Your Answer
Children should not be forced to make hard decisions.			
When hard times come, you should always turn to your family.			
Sports are just like life, and you are the most-valuable player.			
If you don't have the support of your family, you don't have anything.			

Name _____

Date _____

Culminating Activity:
Summary and Verse Book Review

Directions: Write a succinct summary of *The Crossover*. Be sure to include the main characters, setting, and plot of the story.

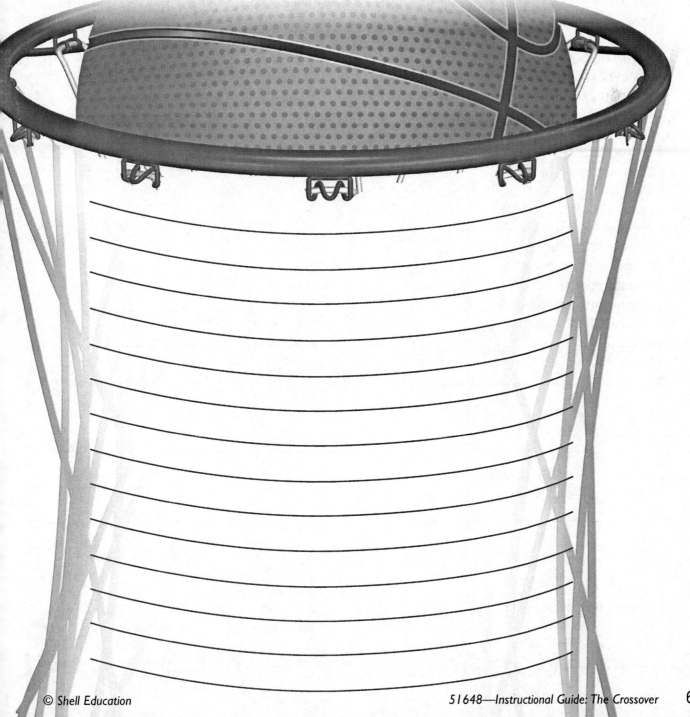

Name _____

Date _____

Culminating Activity:
Summary and Verse Book Review (cont.)

The Crossover by
Kwame Alexander
Is *b r e a t h t a k i n g*.
With trouble lurking in
Shadowy corners.
And deep sadness
Hidden beneath Humor.
Joshua Bell
Has you **hating** him
Loving him
Wishing on stars for him and
Tearing out your hair **for** him.
His brother, JB,
Doesn't have his priorities straight.
In fact, they're so crooked
You want to toss the book
Out the **window**.
For me, the novel started out *s l o w*
But once I kept reading,
It started to *flow*.
I was as hooked as a *fish*.
But then, that horrible
Kwame Alexander
Ripped out my heart
And stomped on it.
This piece was astonishing,
Amazing, and flat out
Beautiful.
I was H
    A
      N
        G
          I
            N
              G
On until the last
Word.

Thank you,
Kwame Alexander
For making me never
Want to read again
Because nothing
Will ever be this
Good.

Directions: Now that you've summarized the story, it's time to write a book review—in verse! To the left is an example verse book review of *The Crossover*. Use the lines to write a rough draft of your own verse book review. Then, recopy your book review and add some artistic embellishments.

_____

_____

_____

_____

_____

_____

_____

_____

_____

_____

_____

_____

_____

_____

Name _____

Date _____

Comprehension Assessment

Directions: Circle the letter for the best response to each question.

1. How does Josh get his nickname?

   A. His room is always *filthy* and *nasty*.

   B. His skills on the court are *nasty*.

   C. His father dedicates a song to him called "Filthy McNasty."

   D. His personality is *nasty*.

2. Which statement supports the reason Josh starts to like his nickname?

   E. "Even Mom had jokes."

   F. "You never clean your closet, and that bed of yours is always filled with cookie crumbs and candy wrappers."

   G. "But, as I got older and started getting game, the name took on a new meaning."

   H. "Only the best song, the funkiest song on Silver's *Paris Blues* album: 'Filthy McNasty.'"

3. There are many similarities and differences between Josh and Jordan. Record a detail for each bullet point in each section of the Venn diagram.

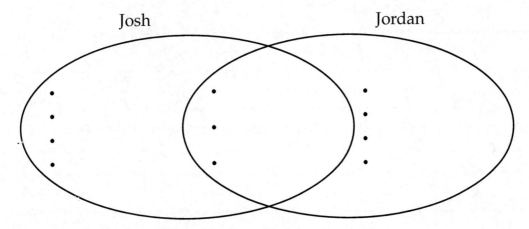

Josh   Jordan

4. Which **two** details listed below could be added to the graphic organizer above?

   A. Josh and Jordan are twins.

   B. They both like Michael Jordan.

   C. Jordan likes to bet.

   D. Both boys have girlfriends.

Comprehension Assessment (cont.)

5. Which of the following can be inferred from this passage in the novel:

   "My father was the light of my world, and now that he's gone, each night is *starless*."

   A. The narrator looks up into the night sky and dreams about his father.

   B. The narrator misses his father, like one would miss the stars in a night sky.

   C. The narrator believes his father is now a star in the night sky.

   D. There aren't any stars in the night sky.

6. The sentence in question 5 is comparing which character to a star?

   E. Josh Bell

   F. Jordan Bell

   G. Dr. Bell

   H. Chuck Bell

7. What is the purpose of this sentence from the novel: "He dribbles back to the top of the key, fixes his eyes on the goal. I watch the ball leave his hands like a bird up high, skating the sky, crossing over us."

   _____

   _____

   _____

8. Why do the boys decide to share their dad's nickname, "Da Man"?

   _____

   _____

   _____

   _____

   _____

   _____

Response to Literature: *The Crossover*

The things you learn by playing sports can be easily connected and applied to themes in everyday life. Kwame Alexander, the author of *The Crossover*, uses basketball as a way to connect to various themes in the novel. One way he does this is with the "Basketball Rules" poems.

Directions: Think about these questions:

- How do the "Basketball Rules" connect basketball and life?
- What symbolism can be found in the poems?
- How do the poems connect to the bigger world or to the characters in the book?
- In what ways can sports be metaphors for life?

Reflect on the "Basketball Rules," and write an essay based on the answers to the preceding questions. Be sure to include evidence from the text. Your essay should follow these guidelines:

- State a clear opinion.
- Write at least 750 words.
- Include answers to all of the above questions.
- Draw upon, directly or indirectly, *The Crossover*.
- Provide a conclusion that summarizes your point.

Name _____

Date _____

Response to Literature Rubric

Directions: Use this rubric to evaluate student responses.

	Exceptional Writing	**Quality Writing**	**Developing Writing**
Focus and Organization	☐ States a clear opinion and elaborates well. Engages readers from the opening hook through the middle to the conclusion. Demonstrates clear understanding of the intended audience and purpose of the piece.	☐ Provides a clear and consistent opinion. Maintains a clear perspective and supports it through elaborating details. Makes the opinion clear in the opening hook and summarizes well in the conclusion.	☐ Provides an inconsistent point of view. Does not support the topic adequately or misses pertinent information. Lacks clarity in the beginning, middle, and conclusion.
Text Evidence	☐ Provides comprehensive and accurate support. Includes relevant and worthwhile text references.	☐ Provides limited support. Provides few supporting text references.	☐ Provides very limited support for the text. Provides no supporting text references.
Written Expression	☐ Uses descriptive and precise language with clarity and intention. Maintains a consistent voice and uses an appropriate tone that supports meaning. Uses multiple sentence types and transitions well between ideas.	☐ Uses a broad vocabulary. Maintains a consistent voice and supports a tone and feelings through language. Varies sentence length and word choices.	☐ Uses a limited and unvaried vocabulary. Provides an inconsistent or weak voice and tone. Provides little to no variation in sentence type and length.
Language Conventions	☐ Capitalizes, punctuates, and spells accurately. Demonstrates complete thoughts within sentences, with accurate subject-verb agreement. Uses paragraphs appropriately and with clear purpose.	☐ Capitalizes, punctuates, and spells accurately. Demonstrates complete thoughts within sentences and appropriate grammar. Paragraphs are properly divided and supported.	☐ Incorrectly capitalizes, punctuates, and spells. Uses fragmented or run-on sentences. Utilizes poor grammar overall. Paragraphs are poorly divided and developed.

The responses provided here are just examples of what the students may answer. Many accurate responses are possible for the questions throughout this unit.

During-Reading Vocabulary Activity—Section 1: Warm-Up (page 16)

1. Josh loves his locked hair, so when Jordan starts to play with it in the car, Josh feels **agitated** and hits Jordan.

2. Jordan is clearly **inspired** by Michael Jordan because he has more than 12 pairs of Air Jordan sneakers and his room is filled with Jordan paraphernalia.

Close Reading the Literature—Section 1: Warm-Up (page 21)

1. At first, Josh thinks the nickname is negative. His mother jokes that his name fits him because his room is always nasty and filthy. He also doesn't like his name at first because kids at school make fun of him.

2. Once Josh's basketball skills start to shine on the court, he begins to love his nickname because it is something his father yells as he cheers for him. It is at the heart of a special bond between the father and son.

3. Josh values his father's opinions very much. His father cheering for him makes him "feel real good about his nickname." Josh likes that his father has a special way to cheer for him.

4. On this page, Kwame Alexander plays with how the words are presented through the fonts and the words themselves. He even smashes words together to create new ones.

During-Reading Vocabulary Activity—Section 2: First Quarter (page 26)

1. JB **taunts** the other players by trash talking them on the court.

2. The boys like to **rummage** through their father's closet and look at his professional basketball paraphernalia. They try on his championship ring and read the articles about "Da Man."

Close Reading the Literature—Section 2: First Quarter (page 31)

1. The boys like going into their parents' closet partially because it's "off-limits." They enjoy seeing their father's paraphernalia from when he played professional ball.

2. JB feels badly about cutting his brother's hair. He realizes that he should not have made that bet and is even willing to do chores as a means of apologizing.

3. The word, "WHOA," is a big hint. Then JB says, "There it is, Filthy." Clearly, they are excited to see it even if they've seen it before. Finally, they whisper as they talk about it and quickly try it on.

4. Readers know from reading this section that Chuck's health is a concern for Dr. Bell. He doesn't listen to his wife about eating healthy. From that, readers can infer that he doesn't listen to what doctors say about his health.

Close Reading the Literature—Section 3: Second Quarter (page 41)

1. Pushing water uphill with a rake is impossible. Chuck is trying to explain to Josh that JB is so distracted by his interest in Alexis that it would be just as impossible to distract him.

2. "Basketball Rule #5" is to never quit playing the way you know how in either life or basketball. If you stop playing your game, then you've already lost. It connects to the twins' relationship. At the moment, they are drifting apart, and Josh wants to prevent that separation.

3. JB seems to be in a daze since he started dating Alexis. Sometimes he ignores Josh, and other times he is daydreaming about her. Even when JB is physically present, Josh thinks he's "not here" because he is thinking about his girlfriend.

4. There are a number of interesting ways that the text is typeset on page 94. "Showoff" has words that are all caps and different sizes. Some words go down the page instead of across the page, and some are spelled in special ways. All of these make the poem able to be read more fluently.

During-Reading Vocabulary Activity—Section 4: Third Quarter (page 46)

1. Josh is **disciplined** by his parents. He is suspended from basketball and is not able to help his team earn a spot in the championship.

2. Josh's **distractions** include his relationship with his brother, his father's illness, being suspended from the team, and feeling isolated.

Close Reading the Literature—Section 4: Third Quarter (page 51)

1. Josh writes an apology letter because JB is ignoring him. On page 148, Chuck suggests to Josh that a letter might be the only way to reach JB right now.

2. Josh compares the brothers' relationship to a "goal with no net," "shattered, like puzzle pieces on the court," "two stars stealing sun," and "two brothers burning up."

3. Josh's analogies all have to deal with loss or being incomplete. This is how he feels at the moment because JB is no longer speaking to him. Ever since JB got distracted by Alexis, the brothers' relationship hasn't been as strong as it used to be. When Josh hurt JB, it got worse.

4. There are two clues that indicate JB has read the letter. First, he laughs on the bus when Josh makes a corny joke. Secondly, Alexis glares at Josh across the cafeteria. She is just being protective of JB, but she may also know that Josh is trying to get his brother to come back to him.

Close Reading the Literature—Section 5: Fourth Quarter and Overtime (page 61)

1. Alexander writes, "He's no longer listening to music, but his tears are loud enough to dance to." This hyperbolic statement exaggerates JB's tears to reflect how hard he is crying.

2. Throughout the book, there are two things that have been made very clear about Josh: He lives and breathes basketball, and he has a very close relationship with his father. So, in the moment when he has to decide what to do, he thinks of what his father would do and follows his gut. JB has never put basketball first throughout the book. He loves the game, but he understands that it is just one part of his life.

3. Josh is getting through the game only because of his love for his father. Their joint passion over the sport is pushing him to help his team win. However, in the back of his mind, he is thinking over all the indicators from the past few months that his dad is really sick. He knows that his dad is in trouble, and he wants to stop bad things from happening.

4. Josh hits the game-winning basket with tears rolling down his face. His team has won the championship, but the words "Game/over" also indicate that his father has passed away. That phrase has two meanings in this situation.

Comprehension Assessment (page 67)

1. C. His father dedicates a song to him called "Filthy McNasty."

2. G. "But, as I got older and started getting game, the name took on a new meaning."

3. Josh: can dunk, thinks only of basketball, forward, dreads, plays in championship game. Both: play basketball, live with their mom and dad, lose their father.
   Jordan: obsessed with Michael Jordan, has a girlfriend, doesn't play in championship game, plays guard

4. A. Josh and Jordan are twins.;
   C. Jordan likes to bet.

5. B. The narrator misses his father, like one would miss the stars in a night sky.

6. H. Chuck Bell

7. These last sentences in the book leave one final crossover reference for readers. Symbolically, being "up high" can represent that Chuck is still watching over them from above, even though he is gone.

8. Nicknames have been a central theme in the book. The twins receive their nicknames from family members. They are signs of love and rites of passage. Now that Chuck has passed away, taking his nickname symbolizes that each boy may now have to fill his shoes and watch over the family.